TOM HOLLAND

Biography of the Spider-Man

Info Edge

This book was presented to

Holly

On Friday 22nd July 2022

By New Road Primary School

Good Luck at Ryburn Holly

CONTENTS

Title Page

Copyright

Early Life   1

Personal Life   3

Early Career   4

As Spiderman   7

Amazing Facts   14

Bonus Info   16

Thank You   19

                                             21

Tom Holland - The SpiderMan

EARLY LIFE

Thomas Stanley Holland was brought into the world on 1 June 1996 in the town of Kingston upon Thames, England to photographic artist Nicola (née Frost) and Dominic Holland, a comic, and creator. He has three more youthful siblings. His fatherly grandma was from Tipperary, Ireland.

Holland was instructed at Donhead, a Catholic private academy in Wimbledon in South West

London, trailed by Wimbledon College, a willful supported Jesuit complete school, up until December 2012. He was harassed in school for being an artist. After Wimbledon College, he went to the BRIT School for Performing Arts and Technology in Croydon. During a break in his vocation in his late adolescents, Holland momentarily went to carpentry school in Cardiff, Wales.

PERSONAL LIFE

Holland dwells in Kingston upon Thames in southwest London, close to the place of his folks and more youthful siblings. He has a blue Staffordshire Bull Terrier named Tessa. He was determined to have dyslexia at age seven. He is an ally of Tottenham Hotspur.

EARLY CAREER

Holland started moving at a hip bounce class at Nifty Feet Dance School in Wimbledon. He hit the dance floor with his school bunch at the 2006 Richmond Dance Festival, where he was spotted by choreographer Lynne Page, a partner to Peter Darling, choreographer of Billy Elliot and Billy Elliot the Musical. After eight tryouts and two ensuing long stretches of preparing, on 28 June 2008, Holland made his West End debut in Billy

Elliot the Musical as Michael Caffrey, Billy's dearest companion. He gave his first execution in the lead spot on 8 September 2008, getting positive takes note. Holland originally educated aerobatic during his time acting in the melodic.

In September 2008, Holland (along with co-star Tanner Pflueger) gave his first TV meet, on the news program on channel FIVE. The accompanying 31 January, he was on the debut of the ITV1 show The Feel Good Factor, during which he played out a form of "Furious Dance" from Billy Elliot the Musical, alongside Pflueger and Layton Williams, two different entertainers who were playing the lead spot, and was met by have Myleene Klass. For the last The Feel Good Factor on 28 March 2009, he prepared five British students for a dance schedule.

On 8 March 2010, to stamp the fifth commemoration of Billy Elliot the Musical, Holland and three other current Billy Elliots were welcome to 10 Downing Street to meet Prime Minister Gordon Brown. Holland was picked to be a pioneer at the fifth-commemoration show on 31 March 2010. He pivoted with three different entertainers in the lead spot of Billy Elliot the Musical until 29 May 2010.

In 2011, Holland was projected in the British name of the enlivened dream film Arrietty, delivered by Japan's Studio Ghibli. He gave a voice to the chief person Sho. Holland made his component movie debut in The Impossible (2012), coordinated by J.A. Bayona, close by Naomi Watts and Ewan McGregor.

The film debuted at the Toronto International Film Festival on 9 September 2012 and was a basic and business achievement, procuring $180.3 million around the world. Holland got widespread recognition from pundits and won a few honors, including the National Board of Review Award for Breakthrough Performance and the London Film Critics Circle Award for Young British Performer of the Year.

He featured as Isaac in the dramatization film How I Live Now, which was delivered in the UK on 4 October 2013, co-featuring Saoirse Ronan. Holland likewise loaned his voice in a supporting job for the dramatization film Locke (2013), featuring Tom Hardy, and showed up in Billy Elliot the Musical Live (2014) to praise his job as a 'previous Billy'.

AS SPIDERMAN

In 2015, Holland showed up in four episodes of BBC Two's verifiable miniseries Wolf Hall, as Gregory Cromwell, child of the hero Thomas Cromwell played by Mark Rylance. He likewise co-featured as Thomas Nickerson in the movie In the Heart of the Sea (2015), coordinated by Ron Howard. On 23 June 2015, it was reported that Holland was given a role as an adolescent Peter Parker/Spider-Man, and his "life was turned over", as he later tweeted, as a feature of a six-picture manage Marvel Studios. As a feature of the Marvel Cinematic Universe (MCU), he initially showed up as Spider-Man in Captain America: Civil War (2016). The film was an enormous basic and business achievement, netting more than $1.1 billion around the world, making it the most noteworthy earning film of 2016, with Holland getting basic acclaim.

In 2016, he played Bradley Baker in the film Edge of Winter, where he co-featured with Joel Kinnaman and Percy Hynes White. In 2017, Holland co-featured close by Charlie Hunnam in the dramatization movie The Lost City of Z, coordinated by James Gray, and delivered in April, to positive basic gathering. Holland additionally proceeded as the on-set substitute for the personality of The Monster as he would rejoin with chief J.A. Bayona in the film A Monster Calls (2016). Entertainer Liam Neeson gave the voice to the person, while Holland was credited with an extraordinary much obliged.

In 2017, the 20-year-old Holland won the BAFTA Rising Star Award at the 70th British Academy Film Awards, turning into the second-most youthful champ of the honor, after British entertainer Bakery, who won it at 19.

He later co-featured close by Richard Armitage and Jon Bernthal in the film Pilgrimage. The film debuted on 23 April 2017 at the Tribeca Film Festival, in its "Perspective" segments. Likewise that year, Holland played Samuel Insull close by Avengers co-star Benedict Cumberbatch in Alfonso Gomez-

Rejon's The Current War, which debuted at the Toronto International Film Festival. Early audits of The Current War were blended, however Holland's presentation got acclaim. In May 2017, Holland showed up with Zendaya on Paramount Network's Lip Sync Battle, during which he played out a dance number to Rihanna's "Umbrella".

July 2017 brought the arrival of Spider-Man: Homecoming, in which Holland repeated his job from Captain America: Civil War. Homecoming got positive audits and Holland significant recognition, with his exhibition called "a star execution was given by a conceived entertainer." The film earned more than $800 million around the world. His presentation procured Holland a Guinness Book of World Records recorded as the most youthful entertainer to play a lead spot in the MCU.

Holland repeated Spider-Man in Avengers: Infinity War, delivered on 27 April 2018, and afterward in that film's development, Avengers: Endgame, delivered on 26 April 2019. He started shooting the continuation Spider-Man: Far From Home in July 2018, with creation wrapping that October. The film was delivered worldwide on 2 July 2019. The trailer was first displayed at Sony's CCXP Brazil board on 8 December 2018, with Holland and Jake Gyllenhaal, who depicts Mysterio, in participation to advance the film.

Holland next co-featured with Will Smith in the Blue Sky Studios energized film Spies in Disguise, voicing the film's leads, which was delivered in

December 2019. In 2020, Holland voiced Jip, a canine, in the surprisingly realistic film Dolittle, close by his MCU co-star. He then, at that point, had the lead voice job of Ian Lightfoot, a mythical person, inverse Avengers co-star Chris Pratt, in the Pixar energized film Onward. Holland next featured in The Devil All the Time, a spine chiller set post-World War II, close by his Avengers co-star Sebastian Stan. The movie, delivered in September 2020, was coordinated by Antonio Campos and created by Gyllenhaal.

Holland featured Chaos Walking, a variation of Patrick Ness' top of the line sci-fi series of a similar name close by Daisy Ridley. He plays Todd Hewitt. The movie was coordinated by Doug Liman and is dispersed by Lionsgate. After helpless test screenings, he returned for reshoots, and the film was delivered on 5 March 2021. In March 2019, it was affirmed that Holland was given a role as the lead job in Cherry, in view of the novel of similar name, reteaming him with his Avengers chiefs, the Russo siblings. Cherry was delivered in films on 26 February 2021 and carefully on Apple TV+ on 12 March 2021.

In November 2021, Holland voiced Percy Pig in Marks and Spencer's Food Christmas notice. In December 2021, Spider-Man: No Way Home, Holland's third MCU Spider-Man film and a film where his Spider-Man archetypes Tobey Maguire and Andrew Garfield additionally featured as their emphasess of the person close by him, was delivered.

In May 2017, it was declared that Holland had been given a role as a youthful Nathan Drake in the 2022 film variation of Naughty Dog's Uncharted computer game series. Head photography started on 16 March 2020, shooting in Berlin, which enclosed by October 2020. He is additionally given a role as the lead job in the transformation of Beneath a Scarlet Sky with Amy Pascal's creation organization Pascal Pictures delivering.

In 2016, Holland was projected in The Modern Ocean, a trial epic by essayist chief Shane Carruth. Holland referred to it as "the best content I've at any point perused". The task has experienced improvement issues, with Holland set for a supporting job close by a group cast with Keanu Reeves, Daniel Radcliffe, Anne Hathaway, Jeff Goldblum, Chloë Grace Moretz, Asa Butterfield, Abraham Attah, and Irrfan Khan. Since Carruth declared his retirement and delivered the full content and the incomplete score, the task is probably not going to start creation at any point in the near future. Holland was additionally pushing for a lead job in Sam Mendes' 1917 in September 2018 at the end of the day was not involved as he was legally committed to do reshoots for Chaos Walking in April 2019 with the lead job at last going to George MacKay. In 2020, Holland guaranteed in a BBC Radio 1 meeting that he was drawn closer by an anonymous maker about a potential reboot of the Back to the Future establishment with him featuring the lead job as Marty McFly (or a comparative new person), however said he was hesitant to take up this proposal as he depicted the current movies as 'amazing movies', however he would be keen on re-causing situations from the movies in a profound phony praise video or short film. In 2021 while advancing the film Cherry, Holland uncovered he had additionally tried out for the job of Finn in the Star Wars continuation set of three preceding John Boyega was projected.

Holland has said that he might want to "do a few additional establishments" and play "a few meatier independent jobs and eventually...transition to the opposite side of the camera and branch into coordinating." In a meeting distributed in November 2021 with GQ, Holland cast question on whether he would repeat his job as Peter Parker/ Spider-Man in future Spider-Man film projects after No Way Home recommending the opportunity might arrive for him to continue on and that it proposed he will have "accomplished something wrong" assuming he kept on playing the person into his 30s. He said he might want to see a surprisingly realistic Spider-Man film story with Miles Morales in the mantle rather than Parker. Nonetheless, maker Amy Pascal expressed her longing to keep Holland in the job. Holland's Spider-Man co-star Jacob Batalon has additionally recommended to MovieWeb that Holland would be keen on succeeding Daniel Craig in the job of James Bond with Holland himself staying demure regarding the matter. In December

2021, he affirmed that he will play Fred Astaire in a biopic at present being developed at Sony.

AMAZING FACTS

He is oldest of four young men.

Tom is a Gemini, conceived June 1, 1996.

Despite the fact that he has an ideal American articulation as Peter Parker, Tom is from London, England.

He was determined to have dyslexia when he was a youngster.

He is an artist and athlete.

He loves Arsenal Football Club.

He cherishes playing golf.

As a child, he was tormented for being an artist.

Tom is companions with his Avengers co-star Robert Downey Jr. also the two as of late went climbing.

Tom is most popular for his job as Peter Parker/ Spider-Man in the most recent Spider-Man and Avengers films. He continues in the enormous strides of individual Brit Andrew Garfield, and Tobey Maguire before him.

Both Tobey Maguire and Tom Holland are 5'8".

Andrew Garfield is 5'10".

To separate himself from the opposition while trying out for the pined for job, Tom did a reverse somersault to intrigue the makers and projecting chief. That is devotion!

Tom was projected in Billy Elliot the Musical on London's West End in 2008 as Billy's closest companion Michael and later proceeded to play Billy. He was projected in the melodic in the wake of being found for his moving by a projecting chief.

Tom showed up in his first element film The Impossible close by Ewan McGregor and Naomi Watts about the 2004 Indian Ocean torrent in Thailand.

He got a Hollywood Spotlight Award for his presentation in The Impossible.

He has broken his nose two times while shooting various motion pictures.

He as of now has seven undertakings in progress including three vivified motion pictures where he voices characters.

His more youthful siblings are a bunch of twins (Sam and Harry) and afterward the most youthful sibling, Paddy.

His father is a jokester and entertainer named Dominic.

BONUS INFO

Tom Holland was tormented for his appreciation for moving at Donhead. It was in Wimbledon College that he would begin learning and moving. In one of the projects, he was spotted by Choreographer Lynne Page who in a flash perceived his ability in moving. He encouraged Tom to give a tryout for the Billy Elliot Musical from that point his moving vocation started that in the long run progressed into acting. He additionally went to BRIT school of performing expressions and innovation where he mastered acting and moving.

He played Lucas in his first film "The inconceivable". He was selected the "Best New Actor" in the GOYA grants in 2012 for Impossible. Furthermore won the ER Rising Star grant in the BAFTA 2017. The significant jump in his profession was the point at which he featured in the Avengers Movie "Commander America: Civil War" as Peter Parker which was his youth dream.

The fans were charmed with regards to the baffling little fellow in the Civil War as all were familiar with seeing more adult projects like Tobey Maguire and Andrew Garfield. He needed to counterfeit his inflection and nobody acknowledged He was not American. This gave Marvel genuinely necessary clout to chip away at their future continuation Homecoming to appropriately acquaint their agreeable neighborhood spiderman with the world.

Other than Avengers he likewise worked in notable motion pictures like The Current War, in 2017 he played a pioneer in the lost city of Z and a Novice Monk in the Movie Pilgrimage.

The Young entertainer needs to turn into a Movie Director later on.

THANK YOU

Printed in Great Britain
by Amazon

82711154R00020